The Master of Insomnia

The Master of Insomnia
Selected Poems
Boris A. Novak

With an Introduction by Aleš Debeljak

**Translated by
Michael Biggins, Mia Dintinjana,
Evald Flisar, Richard Jackson,
Erica Johnson Debeljak, Boris A. Novak,
Lili Potpara, Andrew Wachtel,
and Irena Zorko**

DALKEY ARCHIVE PRESS
CHAMPAIGN • DUBLIN • LONDON

Library of Congress Cataloging-in-Publication Data

Novak, Boris A.
  [Mojster nespecnosti. English]
  The master of insomnia : selected poems / Boris A. Novak ; with an introduction by Aleš
Debeljak ; translated by Michael Biggins ... [et al.]. -- 1st ed.
    p. cm.
  ISBN 978-1-56478-783-5 (pbk. : alk. paper)
  I. Debeljak, Aleš, 1961- II. Title.
  PG1919.24.O8M6413 2012
  891.8'416--dc23
                        2012021659

Partially funded by a grant from the Illinois Arts Council, a state agency

In cooperation with the Slovene Writers' Association – Litterae Slovenicae Series

This project has been funded with support from the European Commission. This publication re-
flects the views only of the author, and the Commission cannot be held responsible for any use
which may be made of the information contained therein.

This work has been published with the support of the Trubar Foundation, located at the Slo-
vene Writers' Association, Ljubljana, Slovenia

This translation has been financially supported by the Slovenian Book Agency

Cover: design and composition by Mikhail Iliatov

www.dalkeyarchive.com

Printed on permanent/durable acid-free paper and bound in the United States of America

CONTENTS

INTRODUCTION
THE SLEEPLESSNESS AND POETRY OF WITNESS

ALEŠ DEBELJAK

A distinct image, a fragment of memory: I stand in the foyer of the splendidly dilapidated Kazina Palace in the center of Ljubljana, the capital city of Slovenia. The palace houses the offices of the fortnightly student publication *Tribuna*, of which I was the editor in the early 1980s. The newspaper was one of the few independent intellectual forums in Slovenia.

But wait, hold your horses! What is Slovenia?

Slovenia was in the 1980s one of the six constituent republics of what was a larger federal state, Yugoslavia. Except for a few political experts, academics, and adventuresome German, Italian, and British tourists, nobody in the West really knew then what Slovenia was or what its culture was like. In the fog of the Cold War, it was only a marginal part of East European *terra incognita*, but today the country is an independent nation-state and a member of the European Union. Thus, a brief outline of the vagaries of Slovenian collective existence is perhaps in order.

In July 1991, Slovenia made the headlines all over the Western world. Its mercifully brief "Ten-Day War," together with the larger convulsions of the Yugoslav breakup, brought about a major change on the map of Europe. Riding on the heels of the disintegrated Soviet Union, the end of the communist *ancien régime*, and German unification, Slovenia held a public referendum, rooted in the natural right to self-determination, which formed the legal foundation for its seeking independence from the moribund Yugoslav Federation. For the first time in the history of this tenacious Southern Slavic people, Slovenians were free to live in a state of their own. This event had been hoped for and, against all odds, anticipated by many Slovenian writers for years.

ROMANTIC FOUNDATIONS

As in other Central and East European countries, writers in Slovenia were traditionally invested with the obligation and the attendant risk to act as the keepers of the national flame, guardians of our moral, social, and spiritual values. Specifically, it was the language itself that represented our most cherished national treasure. Why? Because Slovenians lacked full-fledged political, economic, or social institutions that would have helped maintain a sense of national unity. Naturally, this sense tends to be better developed in countries that have—at least historically—attained some form of statehood or another. Slovenians have been less fortunate. They've lived under royalist, fascist, and communist regimes, respectively, as they failed to reach a goal to which all European regions aspired: statehood.

But the Slovenian people, its language, and its books were around long before the independent Republic of Slovenia was established. Squeezed in between the Germanic, Italian, and Hungarian cultures, and ruled by often predatory political regimes, the Slovenian language was more or less the only buffer against the threat of collective obliteration. Small wonder that today six thousand books are published annually for and by a tiny population of two million, an industry in which "elite" poetry collections routinely come out in editions of five hundred, while "popular" books of verse may be published in editions of up to three thousand.

The forests that cover more than fifty percent of Slovenia continue to provide raw material for printers, just as the contradictions of its collective life continue to provide material for its literary achievements.

These achievements arise out of processes long underway. The dominant one must be seen in a history that lacks splendid military victories but is replete with linguistic resistance to foreign rule. For all practical purposes, Slovenian history is the history of the Slovenian language. It is a language that, in addition to singular and plural, also uses a rare dual form. In other words, it's made for intimate, personal, and erotic confessions.

Although written records in Slovenian (sermons, confessions, poems) had appeared sporadically from the eighth century on, these were little more than fragments. It was fifty years of Protestant Reformation that gave Slovenians a systematic orthography, alphabet, and standardized language. The first book in Slovenian appeared in 1550, one of twenty-two that would be written by the father of Slovenian literature, Primož Trubar: a Protestant preacher who had fled to Germany from the religious persecution in his native land. Thanks to his efforts, Slovenians could read the Old and New Testaments in their mother tongue half a century before the publication of King James Bible.

However, after the aggressive Counter-Reformation, it was Roman Catholicism that became the dominant in Slovenia religion. Its entrenchment in our culture was facilitated by the

Habsburgs, the Catholic rulers of the Austrian—later Austro-Hungarian—Empire to which Slovenia traditionally belonged. The Napoleonic regime came between 1809 and 1813. The French instituted the teaching of the Slovenian language in elementary schools, promoting it as the idiom of the middle class to an extent that would have been inconceivable under the German-speaking Habsburgs. The relentless pressure of Germanic culture and continuous political subjugation made it difficult to envision Slovenia's survival as a discrete entity. The oft-spoken prediction of the time was that the Slovenians would pass into oblivion as a distinct ethnic community. But early in the nineteenth century, Slovenian literary journals began to be published in Ljubljana, the focal point of modern Slovenian life. National self-awareness reached its predictable peak in Romanticism, neck and neck with other Central and East European peoples.

The work of France Prešeren (1800–1849), perhaps the most celebrated Slovenian poet, best encapsulates the community's longing for freedom and independence. Admittedly, his work in English translation sounds like derivative Byronism, but for Slovenians, Prešeren is paramount. A free-thinking lawyer, he wrote in German, the Central European *lingua franca*, as fluently as in Slovenian. Slovenian, however, was more than his mother tongue. It was his language of choice, signaling his political commitment. Prešeren is thus more than a literary icon. He's the founding father of modern Slovenian self-understanding. He addressed all Slovenians and prompted them to recognize themselves as members of a single community, beyond their attachments to various regions of their largely rural existence.

Prešeren's "Zdravljica" ("A Toast to Freedom") is today the Slovenian national anthem. Back in the 1840s, the censors in imperial Vienna correctly identified the revolutionary potential in this poem in which Prešeren called for the unification of all Slovenians and the necessary defense of their independence, up to and including the use of violence, resulting in its being excluded from Prešeren's one published book of poems. Despite this, and despite the fact that *Poezije* sold pathetically—a mere thirty-odd copies in Prešeren's lifetime—he nonetheless managed to accomplish two historic feats: a symbolic unification of the Slovenian ethnicity and the radical invention of its high aesthetic standards. In poems where national and individual destinies blend into a universal message of freedom, Prešeren transformed his mother tongue from a means of expression into the political foundation of national identity.

The disintegration of the Austro-Hungarian Empire in 1918 compelled Slovenians to make a pivotal choice: either go it alone, a route for which they were ill-equipped, or else seek refuge in yet another collective state—that is, together with the other Southern Slavs (except the Bulgarians). The die was cast. The Kingdom of Serbs, Croats, and Slovenians became their common home. It was later renamed Yugoslavia.

Its vibrant cultural life reflected the aesthetic trends of Paris and Vienna, Munich and Prague. Literary debates on expressionism, constructivism, and surrealism were, however, imbued with a political hue. This uneasy bond between politics and literature became a question of life and death after the Nazi invasion of Yugoslavia in April 1941.

Having lost credibility, the royal family and its government fled into exile. Most, though not all, writers joined the anti-Nazi guerrilla units, the Partisans. They printed their books, newspapers, and magazines in makeshift print shops, set up in liberated rural and forested areas. They organized literary readings, published periodicals, and, by design, engaged in nationalist and communist propaganda.

AFTER THE SECOND WORLD WAR

The Partisan resistance proved victorious. After the War, several writers rose in the Yugoslav political hierarchy. A renowned poet, a high-ranking partisan and Christian Socialist, Edvard Kocbek (1904–1981) was a minister in the federal Yugoslav government until he fell out of favor. Educated in Slovenia and France, Kocbek was the first to expose the most fiercely guarded communist secret: that the war of liberation was, to a considerable degree, a civil war as well. Simultaneous with the anti-Nazi struggle, a tragic fratricidal war of "reds" (communist-led partisans) against "whites" (Axis-collaborators), took place primarily in and around Ljubljana.

After the War, uniformed collaborationists and their civilian sympathizers retreated to the Allied-controlled southern Austria. The Allies under British command returned them to Yugoslavia. There, up to twelve thousand people were soon thereafter indiscriminately killed by special units of Josip Broz Tito's communist regime. Against the official imperative of silence, Kocbek's was a dissenting voice. He publicly denounced this criminal act of wild vengeance. The poet ultimately won over the statesman. Kocbek thus remained indebted to the legacy of Prešeren. Only after a loss of direct access to the mechanisms of power was Kocbek able to tell the complete truth. In a way, the civil war was a reflection of traditional antagonism between secular liberalism and Roman Catholic conservatism, the two major mental paradigms in Slovenian history. A dangerous though crucial subject, it occupied many writers throughout the communist years, even though it necessitated the use of Aesopian allegories, designed to fool the regime's censors. The late fifties and the early sixties saw an outburst of creative activity. New literary journals were established. They gradually became strongholds of independent thought, facilitating the growing political dissent that in 1964 exploded in a massive popular protest.

The communist leaders put these demonstrations down, banned the magazines, and arrested several people, including Tomaz Šalamun (1941–), who is today the most internationally admired Slovenian poet. At the time, however, he was a fledgling *enfant terrible* with many parodies of canonical patriotic poems to his credit. Šalamun's talent for poetic absurdity, irony, and playfulness made it possible for him to declare, following his spiritual godfather Arthur Rimbaud, that all dogmatic tradition is the "game . . . of countless idiotic generations." His contested emancipation of verse from under the shackles of obsessive, single-minded nationalism had far-reaching consequences for the nascent autonomy of Slovenian writing.

As a result of the political clampdown, the writers of the '70s retreated from the public arena to rediscover "language as the house of being." They explored the limits of lyrical and narrative techniques, the vertigo of linguistic transgressions, the abandonment of coherent plots. In these works, irony and poetic absurdity were employed as protection against, not as a challenge to, the external reality.

After a decade of passivity, the patience of our intellectuals wore thin. The early 1980s saw the launching of another new magazine, and the reviving of public literary debate. Called—appropriately—*Nova revija* (The New Review), the poems, novels, testimonies, and short stories published in its pages helped to gradually peel off the layers of institutional lies. The leading poetic voice was that of Dane Zajc (1921–2005), a doyen of dark premonitions. The horrors of Titoism, a political system then much admired among the Western left, were laid bare.

In the larger Yugoslav state, Serbian political appetites began to be seen as a threat to the other nations in the federation. The communist-dominated Serbian government took over the federal administration, appropriated more than half of the federal hard currency reserves, attempted to alter the educational curriculum in favor of Serbian authors, and imposed brutal apartheid on ethnic Albanians in Kosovo. Slovenia called for a political cohabitation that would satisfy the constituent nations but retain the Yugoslav frame. The increasingly arrogant Belgrade authorities, alas, glibly dismissed the possibility of compromise. Slovenia had to choose: either remain under the heel of a corrupt communist authority or establish an independent state.

Following passionate public debates, writers led the democratic opposition in drafting the declaration of Slovenian independence. Stimulated by such actions, even the Slovenian communists began resisting the centralized government in Belgrade. After a public referendum, the independent nation-state of Slovenia was declared in July 1991. The Ten-Day War ensued. Despite the shortness of the conflict, it was by no means small: it spiraled into brutal excesses that engulfed the entire region, and hostilities still simmer beneath the surface of the ex-Yugoslav states, despite the Dayton accords in 1995 that nominally ended the wars for Yugoslav succession.

But now, at last, back to *Tribuna*. Tito, the undisputed leader of Yugoslavia, died in 1980. The decade between his death and up to the Yugoslav breakup in 1991 was marked by the rise of civil society and an increased critique of the communist regime. The student paper I was editing at the time eagerly joined the fray. *Tribuna* was guided by youthful naïveté and a dissident attitude that didn't take long to incur the wrath of the communist authorities. The paper was brought under the close scrutiny of government censors, and the editors were assigned "shadows," secret policemen meant to scare us off the task at hand.

So, standing beside me in the foyer of Kazina Palace one day was a bespectacled and black-bearded poet, nodding with understanding of and support for my commitment to both *Tribuna*'s politics and my own creative ambitions in poetry. Even today I can vividly remember the gentle, soothing tone of his voice and the confident though not self-aggrandizing things he said. He spoke as a man with both experience and faith, as a man who had followed the "moral imperative" within him as well as the starry sky above.

I trusted this poet, in short, because I felt I understood him— though he was a generation senior to me. I liked his writing and his many lyrical translations and was impressed by his performances at the numerous informal critical groups that made up literary life.

His name was Boris A. Novak.

Novak was then chief editor of *Nova Revija*. Gathered around this monthly magazine were most, if not all, of the best and brightest in the Slovenian intellectual community. Novak's leadership coincided with the period of a government crackdown on *Nova Revija*, which had become a serious thorn in the side of the ruling elite. Despite pressure on him exerted through both informal channels and mass media campaigns of character assassination, Novak never abandoned his commitment to the political ideals of an open and democratic society.

Novak's attitude was shaped by his immersion in two cultures and two languages, the byproduct of a childhood spent in the then-capital of Yugoslavia, Belgrade, a Serbo-Croat-speaking city. Novak was born in Belgrade in 1953 and attended elementary school there. His adolescent arrival in Slovenia necessitated a rediscovery of his mother tongue. His family's urbane tolerance and his father's past as a high-ranking officer in the Partisan antifascist movement during the Second World War are all prominent forces that cemented Novak's commitment to the universal, if utopian, values of solidarity, equality, and brotherhood.

SHOW OF SOUND AND MEANING

No less important, however, Novak never abandoned his commitment to the idiosyncratic aesthetics of sound and meaning, which he propelled to ever more beautiful heights. Novak's first book of poems, *Stihožitje* (Still Life with Verses), was published in 1977;

its untranslatable neologism of a title metaphorically closing the distance between the term *still life* and the magic of verse. This was followed by sixteen further collections to date, most of which have enjoyed the approbation of literary critics and the general reading public alike. In addition to these collections, Novak has published an enviably large number of children's books, puppet and radio plays, and works for the stage. Additionally, Novak assisted in staging numerous plays in the most important theaters in the country, and was employed for several years as a literary adviser at the Slovenian National Theatre.

In his poetry, Novak often explores the aesthetic potential of traditional verse forms, pursuing the mysterious connection between the sounds and meanings of words. Which is to say that he seeks nothing less than poetry's true source. His poetic language successfully appropriates everyday words, using them in new combinations and coaxing unrealized possibilities out of them. He thus allows us to see how extending the limits of what is said can broaden the limits of the known. It was for an innovative paraphrase of the *Arabian Nights—1001 stih* (1001 Verses), a book published in 1983—that the author received the premier literary prize in Slovenia: the Prešeren Award.

BEARING WITNESS

After a year-long teaching stint at the University of Tennessee in Chattanooga, Novak returned home to became president of the Slovenian PEN Center. He led this prestigious organization during the period of escalating conflicts between the republics of the former Yugoslavia, and in the shadow of the increasingly totalitarian ambitions of Slobodan Milošević, who strove to dominate the entire federal entity in the name of all Serbs. This desire for domination eventually led to the eruption of the aforementioned Ten-Day War in the summer of 1991. Then, with a flick of the dragon's evil tail, war swept into Croatia as well, and, later, with particular cruelty, into the towns and villages of Bosnia and Herzegovina.

Novak quickly organized the Slovenian PEN Center as a key distribution point for all the international assistance (collected at national PEN centers around the world) sent to ease the suffering of writers in besieged Sarajevo. Small wonder, then, that Novak responded to the Balkans wars in a poetic idiom: first in his poetry collection *Stihija* (Cataclysm, 1991), and later, at the height of his creative career, in *Mojster nespeϑnosti* (The Master of Insomnia, 1995), which is populated with harrowing images of individual despair in the face of violence. Still, the book exudes an aura of fragile hope, without which its readers might be overwhelmed by apathy and moral indifference. Such moral indifference was a staple in the agendas of many Western governments, a legacy of the brutal realpolitik lodged in European minds since the Munich Agreement of 1938: an earlier episode of the West's failure to rise to a historical challenge. It seems that only poets who speak in their own name and from their own experience are able to respond to such challenges with both aesthetic validity and ethical integrity. Their ethics are revealed or—to be more precise—contained in their poetics.

The following anecdote should illuminate the chasm that yawned between Slovenia's defensive attitude and the militaristic policies of

Serbian national mythology. During the brief period in the summer of 1991 when columns of Yugoslav Army tanks were attacking Slovenian towns and villages, Boris A. Novak sent a letter to the Serbian PEN Center in the hope that he would receive verbal support for the legitimacy of Slovenian resistance against aggression. The response of his literary colleagues in Belgrade was the first, though certainly not the last, great disappointment for Novak during his tenure at PEN. "This is war," came the reply. "During war, people die." An ethical revolt against just this kind of cynicism was what drove Boris A. Novak, despite his own pain, to work tirelessly to help all of those who, in besieged Sarajevo, could not help themselves.

Novak understands that hope and fear provide both individual and collective access to a narrative by which "the soul of generation after generation seeks the way." Hence the necessity for a coherent narrative about the past in order to reach an understanding of the community's present and future. Yet there are two distinct approaches: that of history and that of poetry. Poetry always tells the story of the specific. Thus it is "more true" than history—that is, more accurate that the story of the nonspecific, of the general.

I can think of no reason to doubt this Aristotelian verity. So it's no wonder that, rather than drowning in the supposed neutrality of political economy, and then the fickleness of national rhetoric, I prefer to delve into poetry. I believe that it is possible to find in poetry's lyricism the trembling grace of a special light that can even give meaning to the wars of Yugoslav succession—in much in the same way that this tragedy rewrote, and scarred, the lives of all who live in the region. *The Master of Insomnia* carries such a light. Here the poet successfully weds form to content, achieving an enchanted equilibrium. Hidden within the pages of this book is the key to one of history's great enigmas, which Boris A. Novak slowly reveals before our bewildered eyes.

While a river of Bosnian refugees flowed into the uncertainty of foreign lands, while European diplomats washing their hands like Pontius Pilate became the symbol of the 1990s, while unscrupulous war criminals shook hands with the leaders of "the free world," Novak—as president of the Peace Committee of International PEN (he was appointed to the position in 1994) no less than as a poet—wrote a personal testament of a happy childhood, the only true homeland for the artist. Indeed, the poet dwells in his own ivory tower, but not, as might be conventionally thought, in order to escape the brutal terror of history, but rather to gain the vantage point needed to bear witness.

The poet's personal story is more precise and more revealing than any of the various histories written at strategic institutes or political offices. The poet's voice is singular and doesn't hesitate to utter the existential truth that the individual's story is also the story of the world. He sings with simple and mature beauty: "I am the rapid disintegration of the world."

It's been too long since the poet has slept. Instead he gathers details of unspeakable cruelties and tries to rescue them from oblivion. *The Master of Insomnia* exists because the devastation won't let the poet sleep. He poet doesn't know sleep because he is the witness of the world: not for an instant will he be lured into the magic circle of dreams. His wide-open eyes must watch over both the beauty of this life and the horror of its destruction.

Oscillating between civic engagement and poetic solitude, Novak helped established the Society of the Friends of Lipica, an association tasked with protecting the endangered Lipizzan horse. A co-founder was Monika van Paemel, a Flemish writer. Soon, the two fell in love.

Is there a better method to madness than love? Is there a better way to fend off our catastrophic social-historical reality than with the fragile unity of two souls and bodies? Novak's recent collections, such as *Alba* (1999), testify to the fact that our insomniac poet has found a reinvigorated belief in the possibilities of the good and the beautiful in this most intimate of all human bonds. Having fallen in love with a woman, the poet has mustered his formal skills and lyrical talent to craft a movingly exuberant display of unfettered celebration: celebration of woman, her mystery, and her destiny.

Alba follows in the footsteps of medieval Provençal troubadours—a focus for Novak in his academic career as well—carefully reinventing verse discipline while praising precisely the kind of freedom that knows no limits and is entirely invested in the pursuit of a common joy. It is a jubilant, highly personal, and liberatingly intimate poetic account of two different identities merging into one. However short these moments of unity may be, they are worth preserving in a number of innovative coinings with troubadour roots, including the refrain *alba*, the glow of dawn that greets lovers at the morning farewell.

Saying farewell is, of course, and in a profoundly painful way, just as much a part of the vagaries of love as joy. The past must be embraced, however disfigured. Novak's recent collections, *Žarenje* (Glowing, 2003), *Obredi slovesa* (Rites of Farewell, 2005), and *MOM: Mala Osebna Mitologija* (LPM: Little Personal Mythology, 2007) are clear windows onto Novak's acceptance of the past—his family's and his nation's.

Here, his meditations on the moments of his courtship give way to the kind of poetic discourse that can no longer hide its crucial dependence on social and political reality. The happy unity of the two lovers in *Žarenje* becomes an island under threat. Sinister shadows lurk in the corners and the collective stereotypes of West and East rear their ugly heads as the traces of war and dislocation upon our faces turn into treacherous bromides that help people explain everything and understand nothing.

Novak, a migrant between literary-historical periods and between the "meaning" and "sound" of poetic idiom, has come liberatingly close to accepting migration as a key process that defines the human condition in the contemporary world, shaped as it is by shifting borders and apocalyptic premonitions. Bearing witness to humanity's most evil aspects may be, in the end, the only foundation for the hope that we might to transcend them. Novak's political engagement, personal experience, and, above all, his sophisticated lyrical voice offer such a foundation.

ALEŠ DEBELJAK, 2003–2012

The Master of Insomnia
Selected Poems

THE GARDENER OF SILENCE (1973–75)

*   *   *

A handkerchief is
a white butterfly
of good-bye:

when a landscape moves by,
and a distance comes near,
and a nearness becomes distant,

it trembles, wounded,
over the threshold
of the road:

a white anchor of eyes:
a white source of traces:
a white heart of emptiness.

*   *   *

Every evening the light
gives a bouquet of stars
to the night;

every morning the night
gives a bouquet of shadows
to the light.

*   *   *

Light always enters
without knocking
and leaves
without saying good-bye.

*   *   *

Shadows
are blind,
so the light
takes them
by the hand.

*   *   *

No wind
can touch
the light.

*   *   *

Dawn is a light
shipwrecked
on the reefs
of the night.

*   *   *

Tide
as a rhyme
of the moonlight.

*   *   *

No land
on the horizon . . .
But the eye
is full of islands!

*   *   *

Every sail has its wind,
and every wind its anchor.

*   *   *

The bank wants to catch the river.
The river wants to catch time.
Time wants to catch the bank.

*   *   *

The circle
has lost
its beginning
while searching
for its end.

*   *   *

An echo is a sound
which wants to defeat
its own death.

*   *   *

A monument
is a memory
which had been freezing
so long
until it petrified.

*   *   *

A child in a garden,
the garden in a rose
and the rose in the child's hand,

a game, a childhood of dying!

*   *   *

A poem
enchanted by a rose,
and the rose captured

into the alphabet of its odors,
into the syntax of its colors,
into the speechless vocabulary of its red fear,

when green leaves
change their meaning
and start leaving.

*   *   *

A flower fades
if not watered
by the eyes.

*   *   *

A tree
never forgets
its fallen leaves.

*   *   *

Touch
is a shepherd
of the skin.

*   *   *

Snow was so stunned
by its own whiteness
that it has melted away.

*   *   *

These lines
show
all the whiteness
of the paper.

*   *   *

A poet
is a gardener
of silence.

TRANSLATED BY THE AUTHOR

.

STILL LIFE WITH VERSES (1977)

Still Life with Verses

The flame is undressing a candle and the light is dressing
a room where mirrors reflect each other
and trembling eyes of fire run away
from the immobility of glass deep into the glass infinity.

The voice of a bird is raining from the open cage of time,
and echoing among shadows of shadows,
and dying at the edge of hearing and silence;
in the corner absent fingers are playing the guitar.

In reflecting corridors a woman is flowing,
tender as snow and alive as a melody;
when her skin wants to be fulfilled in a touch
she kisses her own image, cold and distant.

And nothing happens between eyelashes and timelashes;
and nothing does happen: silent happening of nothingness.
Thus life is translated into a still life,
the woman into a desire and the desire into the thirst of language.

TRANSLATED BY THE AUTHOR

A Dream is Snowing

A dream is snowing: behind curtained eyes a garden
waxed by frost, a hole in the airship of sounds,
an aquarium of ancient hours—the night has printed
small, distant lights below eyelids and above
timelids, pearly star-shells in moon sand.

When all the colors brown away and all the shapes sink
into shades, a wizard of darkness, dressed in a cobweb,
translates the world into words and words into birds
cruising above the abyss that is not there.
Portraits are fading away at the edge of oblivion:

in the absent axis of space anchored shadows of women
once touched, under iced cascades of their hair
and voices. And language, drowned somewhere
at the endless bottom of senses, dictates
an underground flow of images to the tongue:

I am a silk zero among fairies of numbers! a tiny mouse
in the tender mechanics of moss! the last letter
in the alphabet of falling! a naked eye drunk
with sand and stones! Let movement be a snake
snaking away from the field of my body!

After each trip to the lottery islands the world refills
emptied senses: the grass is still growing in the sky,
and a cloud is grazing the grass where a rose-verse

is wounded by thorns of its own time: a dream of home
is to be everywhere, a home of dreams is nowhere . . .

TRANSLATED BY THE AUTHOR

Poem

A poem is not a world: it is a pure word,
a birth of the language and the language of the birth in the womb of
  silence.
The poem is not a thing: it is a child of every-thing and no-thing.

The poem is not a light: it is a will for light,
not a fire, but a key of the fire hidden in the night.
The poem is not a woman: it is a silent desire, an embrace of rhymes.

The poem is not a music: it is a naked voice snowing
from the blue sky of hearing to the ceiling of the feeling,
memory of meaning about its childhood so full of sounds.

The poem is not an image: it is a magical mirror.
The poem is not a letter: not by me, it is written by the language itself,
and not to you, it is addressed to everybody and nobody.

And the poem is not a poem: it is a meaning of a meadow and the
  meadow of memory,
memory of the body and the body of no-body: the poem is when it is
  not: sand:
a seed of the unspeakable growing in the paper grass of nothingness,
  without a point

TRANSLATED BY THE AUTHOR

Uni-verse
(erased sonnet)

The light and its night: shapes and their shades,
waves and shores—their graves, and the moon not only full
but fulfilled: and a field—a handful of distance,
and the wind—a fore-finger of the air,
and a bird—a wedding ring of nothing:

and a traveler and his traveling toward the end
of steps, into the root of an endless circle:
a voice, and yet a silence of everything,
the silence, and yet a praise to everything:

touch is the nearest neighbour of the untouchable:
a secret weaving of the birth: a native
death: a mystery of word, a word of mystery:

universe, a unison of unheard star chimes,
universe, an unspeakable rhyme of rhymes,

uni-verse . . .

TRANSLATED BY THE AUTHOR

THE DAUGHTER OF MEMORY (1981)

The Wings of Time
IV. Winter

Winter is a time frozen to total whiteness.
White is the path, white the pathfinder, white the finding of the void.
Silence is white, yet I cannot shade it, for my voice is whiter.
The light is a soft, white silk; the world is a beautiful white
  corpse . . .

But whence so much whiteness? From the white sky.
The horizon? A fiction; unmeasurable, unspeakable whiteness,
no more: whiteness with no bound, no peak, no bottom,
a painful mystery, the first and last . . .

White grass in the fields. Trees with white leaves.
White sheep in a white sleep. Black wolves howling white.
Clouds in a white sky—white, bright, insane stains!
White roofs on houses; inside them, whitened fear . . .

White is the water captured in icy chains;
white the waterfall trapped in midair; white the river with no
  ripples.
White, and void, and beautiful the canvas of this winter scene.
White, and cold, and warm the blanket of the earth as it sleeps, and
  sleeps, and sleeps . . .

White, white are the games: children are snowballs among snow
   balls—
those little bricklayers building a skyscraper of ice,
those little pilots flying on wooden sleds,
those little sculptors cutting ephemeral snowmen . . .

White, white, white is your body! . . . The icy mirror
of the water's surface steals away your white beauty.
Whiteness scrapes beneath our steps as we run out of time!—
The only warmth in this white cold is your white-hot hand . . .

Thy sky's volcano disgorges snow, the eye blinded by white lava.
An avalanche no more than a curl falling from the mountain's old,
   white head.
A white storm wipes out our trails . . . Only a chimney writes in
   black ink,
but the horizon—white sponge—erases its smoky script . . .

It snows . . . white rice at the wedding of sky and earth, sleds of
   dreams.
It snows . . . pulverized whiteness, milk to nurture a child's eye:
a boy melts ice from a window with the warm breath of
   amazement—
and falling whiteness makes him fly, fly, fly high into the sky . . .

A white wind erases space into pure whiteness, a white peace.
Days are short, the nights are long, both are white: time is white.
(I write to blaze a trail through this wintery, white, void paper;
but no use: white are the words, these white words with no
   traces . . .)

This whiteness wiping out all traces . . . this is time snowing within us.

This snow covering all tracks . . . this is death living within us. —
Under its white winter crust a death-bearing river brings a new time:

new springs and summers for us . . . and all of eternity without us . . .

TRANSLATED BY MICHAEL BIGGINS

AND THE AUTHOR

CORONATION (1984)
(wreath of sonnets)

1

Memory has two wings: the first in past, the last in future.
Within us a poppy-smelling grave is growing.
Where a space is too narrow to accept a step
Only voice can dwell in a dead bird's nest.

Our destiny is a freedom of language,
A high spell, a living blood from the time well.
A deep snow of centuries is waiting for us,
Dark of soot, washed out like a fragrant linen.

I am beginning the chant with a great praise to the milk.
A language of milk is whiter than absence.
Word is a womb of the human world.

This poem is beyond power and weakness: only whisper
Kisses a mouth where the river is bound for:
A luxury that hurts, a name of the silence.

2

A luxury that hurts: a name of the silence.
There are fires and eyes burning everywhere.
Irrevocably alone, lost in a sweet confusion,
I am kissing hands to all the people; let it pass.

Let this luxury of the blue pass.
It is enough to be here once, at the edge
Between day and night, tracing signs of death.
The world is rich. I feel like dying of grace.

I have a left and a right hand.
With them I am building a nest for the shapes
Of your body, which is a sea and deep.

The ear is a shell of sounds and silence
In the sand of time sliding through my fingers.
Only dreams can weave time with water.

3

Only dreams can weave time with water.
When everything familiar had strangely changed
A beautiful woman has thrown her shoes into a precipice
Tearing apart a night cobweb with her naked body.

A skirt is a wing shining lonely out of the deep.
(Who is traveling and where to? —Who's asking?)
The beginning of the end. And the end itself? Here it is:
A frightful poem, a sister of the primordial silence.

Destiny is fulfilled exactly as light
In the morning and in the evening. And birds
Fleeing to the south pierce the presence.

Never more. Nowhere. Only little seeds,
Seemingly dead, call the future time,
A magical mirror, a distant face of milk.

4

A magical mirror: a distant face of milk,
Scarcely visible under the magnifying glass.
Sacred waters that haven't broken yet
Shield the fire with the silence of high priests.

When a woman's labor begins a laundress comes
To wash the sky in the light that streams away.
Blood has the strength of steel.
All the things support each other like stairs.

The universe is opened with a birth scream!
The body is a field—the wheat and sickle of the reaper.
Watch: a grain is growing into the highest image.

A trifling grain, smaller than the pupil of the eye,
The same in its desire for the name: the little is great.
Truth is always being born at the edge.

5

Truth is always being born at the edge
Where an utterly sensitive seam
—A mouth of a river kissing a sea—
Is sewn with an invisible thread of the new language.

A prudent palm is making a childbed, celebrating
The body in the rhythm of a dream weaver.
Life is strained like a string on the bow—
On the spin of a sacred woman in labor.

Giving birth is a terrible gift for a woman.
But each and every thing is a tiny thread of a rug
That unites us all into the whole.

Only death undoes our weaving, making a hole
With scissors of emptiness. Under the earth our blood is green.
A child is building the whole world out of clay.

6

A child is building the whole world out of clay.
For him the door is not just a birth of space—
It is the native space itself: the child has to
Open it to become a prince of the wide.

No wall can break time and space.
And the window is not just a bottomless eye
Of the wall—it is the precipice itself that has to
Be opened by each child, each prince of the near . . .

The wardrobe hides an ancient treasure: childhood.
Hidden in folds of skirts, this fragrant,
Tiny, thrilling god will never die.

I've opened the door of my dusty homeland:
Magical tears. —Being grown up I am so poor.
A sand castle is stronger than emptiness.

7

A sand castle is stronger than emptiness.
Invented and ruined by the movement of the moment,
Eternally ancient, it is being renewed and wasted again and again
Under fingers of each and every child, like a fruit.

An immense world is dripping through sensual sieves.
The nearest universe is open to be touched,
A mysterious skin drinking air and sobbing
And hearing only the language of the moist and the warm.

Senses wake up to play with colors and sounds.
A fateful bird of birth is nesting in time,
Filling an empty fist with a palmy kiss.

I am eating the world with an appetite of the spoonful.
The eyes of children are starving for things.
A mother eagle is shielding the calls of the weak ones.

8

A mother eagle is shielding the calls of the weak ones.
Tender games of the beak with a fledgling
Are eternal rites at the peak of the mountain
Where earth rises high, high—to the knees of air.

When a woman carries a sunny seed of the message,
I'm just a man, confused and silent, witnessing
A creation of everything from a crack of nothing.
Her sex is the neck of the broken bottle.

With my palms I am trying to close the burning wound,
The utter sacrifice of the woman's body.
Her skin was never so naked!

A birth is a farewell hurting a child to scream!
We are beings of a bright, native solitude.
Anguish opens like a curtain.

9

Anguish opens like a curtain.
This poem is a moment of silence just before a storm,
Gathering debris of the world torn apart.
Shielded by a wild rhythm I am dancing away from terror.

Mysterious memory is rising higher and higher,
A cypress above the open grave of history.
The sky is enlightened by falling stars,
Wheels of fire, nightmares from a dark childhood of time.

Look, a bulldog with a mouth full of bloody slaver!
When morning begins to mourn and the poem is a curse
And a city is a tower of glass and brass without pity,

Only a child rescues the space with his fresh eyes.
The child is a holiday, a day born out of a hole.
The child is a crown. I crown you, my life.

10

The child is a crown. I crown you, my life.
The whole world is a modest throne for the infant king.
His smile is everything: the greatest hand of light,
Snow for us who are melting snowmen.

The child is created twice: by birth and by the milk.
Breasts are sanctuaries of milky rituals nursing the universe,
A mouth of a sea into a newborn river.
The milk is a pure will, a living water of creation.

Being little the child is living near secrets: he knows by heart
Each and every wrinkle on the wooden face of the furniture.
For him every day is a birthday. A new continent to be discovered.

Only the corner of the eye is sensitive enough to see the weakest
Stars: when you watch them directly they vanish into
The densest moment—terrible is the gold of the body.

11

The densest moment: terrible is the gold of the body,
An ore radiating into nothing, a grain in the flood.
How can a bow still find a color of the sound
Locked deep in the memory of the ear.

After the fire darkness is still darker.
Future days, all those prophetic lights and lies,
Will collapse under the weight of the triumphal arch.
How to rescue a cradle from the earthquake.

A bloody rain will wipe out chalk marks on the blackboard.
A snowman will kill himself melting away.
Only poems still keep the word,

Drawing wings for children to fly.
How to build a house with the mere strength of an eye.
The blooming of the world demands a serene vigil.

12

The blooming of the world demands a serene vigil.
In a poem I am someone who's always missing.
To make a verse sound perfect, I am silent.
To make a flower be perfect, I am fading away.

I am subtracted from the total of everything. —Time is friction.—
The result of the calculation is zero, without a remainder:
The body is a mortal weapon and a mortal wound. Vanishing,
My face is spellbound into the pure vibration of my voice.

I am withdrawing. Now you can watch the field through my ribs.
Nothingness makes me dangerous and vulnerable.
Every fist is full of a terrible will, so I make it a palm.

A change: step here, into the spell of our farewell,
Where I stand. I am no longer there. Instead of me there's a universe.
Here, my child, I bequeath to you all the wonders.

13

Here, my child, I bequeath to you all the wonders.
I, a king of the language, am resigning to the rhymes
Of a royal insensibility, being hurt
By the word. The poem is a body of the body.

I am leaving to you the eyes and strength of the tree,
Laps blossoming in the middle of the winter,
Secrets to hide yourself and call me: I'm not here,
Treasures of sounds and this key of the ear.

I am writing to you with a blue ink of the deep
Where waters of time fall down in a foam.
Don't be afraid. I am a bridge over the fear of heights.

But every peak is a slippery threshold into emptiness.
Don't be afraid—I won't let the world crash the silence of
The knees where I cradle you into floating.

14

The knees where I cradle you into floating
Are flourishing, full of milk, full of nothing.
The lullaby is a soft, sonorous lid
Slowly covering your dreams. Go away, fears.

Learning to rise you're bigger than life.
And you fall down. An immense river always washes away
The world while you're running to become a man
In order to stop the spinning of the earth.

But between yourself and death there is my body
Guarding you. When birds are bound to burn
Only man is free to sing.

Absence will drink out all my eyes.
When you grow up, whisper to this poem: You are mine.
Memory has two wings: the first in past, the last in future.

TRANSLATED BY THE AUTHOR
WITH THE HELP OF RICHARD JACKSON

Sonnet of Sonnets

Memory has two wings: the first in past, the last in future,
A luxury that hurts, a name of the silence.
Only dreams can weave time with water:
A magical mirror, a distant face of milk.

Truth is always being born at the edge:
A child is building the whole world out of clay—
A sand castle is stronger than emptiness.
A mother eagle is shielding calls of the weak ones.

Anguish opens like a curtain.
The child is a crown. I crown you, my life.
The densest moment: terrible is the gold of the body.

The blooming of the world demands a serene vigil.
Here, my child, I bequeath to you all the wonders,
The knees where I cradle you into floating.

TRANSLATED BY THE AUTHOR
WITH THE HELP OF RICHARD JACKSON

THE FORMS OF THE WORLD (1991)
(A Textbook of Poetic Forms)

Night Elegy

All that remains is dust. And dusk. And enormous silence.
 Fear has carved my voice: hush, let me slowly read this line
inscribed in stone, gilded letters that are already fading away.
 This monument is a memory frozen in time
and then petrified, hidden under the moss of oblivion.
 All that remains is nothing. Nothing that remains is nothing.
Nothing that remains is a stone, the wind blowing above the grave,
 an urn full of sleeping ashes, covered by a name.
All that remains is a song. I can hardly read the inscription.
 I can hardly make out the name. It seems familiar.
Where is it from? I tremble at the border between nightmares and day.
 The name, it is mine, my own.

TRANSLATED BY THE AUTHOR
AND ERICA JOHNSON DEBELJAK

CATACLYSM (1991)

The Tower

They build the tower for all eternity, the guardians of the Name,
so the wind won't carry them from this wasted world.
With bare hands, they raise a wall around the flame—
for a great tower, a tower so high it will touch the sky!

So the wind won't carry them from this wasted world,
they erect heavy beams and lift massive stones
for a great tower, a tower so high it will touch the sky.
They don't labor for themselves: they suffer for their sons.

They erect heavy beams and lift massive stones,
and curse their fathers' heritage—mere ruins.
They don't labor for themselves: they suffer for their sons
so their children may drink the golden wine of eternal time.

They curse their fathers' heritage—mere ruins . . .
They grit their teeth, their shoulders waxed by the burning sun,
so their children may drink the golden wine of eternal time.
The tower grows higher and higher but never touches the sky . . .

They grit their teeth, their shoulders waxed by the burning sun.
Above the deep blue abyss, they are gripped by a mysterious fear:
the tower grows higher and higher but never touches the sky . . .

Their eyes bleed and their palms burst into tears . . .

Above the deep blue abyss, they are gripped by a mysterious fear:
debris litters the meadows that lie below them on the distant
     ground.
Their eyes bleed and their palms burst into tears!
They understand now: everything dies, only ruins enjoy eternal
     time . . .

Debris litters the meadows that lie below them on the distant
     ground.
They level the tower and the tower buries their finest sons!
They understand now: everything dies, only ruins enjoy eternal
     time . . .
A sister searches for her brother, a bride cradles the widow's cry!

They level the tower and the tower buries their finest sons,
and the next day dawns without light—only dust and gloom:
a sister searches for her brother, a bride cradles the widow's
     cry . . .
How long must memory flow before moss covers this tomb?

And the next day dawns without light—only dust and gloom...
When they finally see the sky, they begin their labors once again.
How long must memory flow before moss covers this tomb?
And so the curse is repeated forever and then . . .

When they finally see the sky, they begin their labors once again,
with bare hands, they raise a wall around the flame—

and so the curse is repeated forever and then . . .
They build the tower for all eternity, the guardians of the
    Name . . .

TRANSLATED BY THE AUTHOR
AND ERICA JOHNSON DEBELJAK

Absence

Absence surrounds me
like a glass coffin made of air,
silent, fragile dust that lingers
until the end of every step.

Absence reminds me
of an immensely known face,
mysterious as a coffer
sealed by time.

Memory, the only key that unlocks
absence like a bottomless light
gushing from a thousand eyes.

It hurts when I enter it,
my body is so open,
absence, a living death.

TRANSLATED BY ERICA JOHNSON DEBELJAK

Vertigo

The bottom has cracked beneath my feet
like a dark womb of the utter secret,
a magnet inviting me into the hole of madness,
an inborn dread, the voice of a throat just cut.

Obsessed by the childish fear of falling
I cover the abyss with smooth mirrors:
such silver and foam on this ice-field
that all the things glitter like fairy-tale treasures!

Reflecting images multiply the presence
in the narrow space, into the infinity
that is a surface of glass, a surface of the glass scaffold.

I am no longer afraid to stare into the deep.
Now I feel death in the slippery mirror,
in the vertigo of its surface.

TRANSLATED BY THE AUTHOR

The First Poem

I lock myself in the bathroom,
fill the bath with warm, hot water,
undress and stretch into the utter
freedom, into my warm, hot butcher-bed.

Clouds of steam. I hardly find any soap.
And throw it to the wall. Then I search
for a razor. In the very last moment a strange decision
delays the blade for an indefinite time:

to write a poem. Because I'm so hungry
for words. About fear. And grace. And reflections
on the water. About this terrible, beautiful day when I rose
out of my own death. Wet. Naked. Different.

Different eyes are watching me from the mirror.
For this indefinite time that still lasts: thanks.

TRANSLATED BY THE AUTHOR

Southeast of Memory
(little French ballade)

Cruel is the crystal of memory,
cruel when the living call
the dead forcing them
to voice their void—
a sacred, holiday silence
echoing in the winter wind.
Narrow is the skylight ever after:
leave the dead in the dusk!

Words are utterly painful
for the dead:
they prefer to watch buds
southeast of memory.
Hearing a stranger approach
they close their dreamy secrets.
Peaceful is the valley on the other side:
leave the dead in the dusk!

Call the living fields instead!
Let your children call you!
Call the morning, call tomorrow!
Who can understand the whiteness
flowing through the blood of crime?
Who are you to judge field poppies
wiping all the spilled blood?
Leave the dead in the dusk!

The air is too deep.
You will never catch
a shape in the shade.
Leave the dead in the dusk!

TRANSLATED BY THE AUTHOR

THE MASTER OF INSOMNIA (1995)

Past and Present

The past is ever changing.
Only the future stays the same.
No one's. It's blank and strange,
mysterious, an empty chamber.

Whose portrait is this? Whose steps are these?
Amidst the leaves, whose names on graves?
After the leaves fall, rulers rend memories,
to brush them away.

The past is ever changing,
shaded in by memory's brush,
but future's sky is clear.

It can't be rearranged.
Completely mine and fresh,
it closes overhead, an empty chamber.

TRANSLATED BY ANDREW WACHTEL

Black Hole

Never has the page before me
been so white and empty.
Silent with grief, I am running from the wound
where the world trembles and is rent asunder.
The air is already full of words,
that fall on paper like black soot.
Yet silence is even deadlier.
That's why with my knees I write a dusty trace
of prayer, which is swallowed by the evening . . .

The heart, intoxicated by the winds,
has been broken among the faces
of the gods, to whom it was sacrificed
for food, in an abyss where this fast epoch
was born and is now ending,
bloody, alone, and ours: and nothing
will there ever be again, only unrest,
which shuts up the lids of so many eyes . . .
I am being sucked into a black hole; and the cloth

is bloody . . . There is someone who
can cut fateful lines into the forehead,
our gift to the day, with complete composure.
Someone who pulls fragile vases of
bodies from God's hands and crumbles them in his fist.
And there is someone who through a telescope
is catching the eyes of children, still full of stars,

to kill the open, growing look! . . .
But on the other side of war: market, ice, derision . . .

Why, with my knees, do I write the dusty trace of prayer?
I know that I, too, am part of this war,
however safe on the margin of the Earth.
Words are swallowed by ever-greater shadows,
and I am being sucked into a black hole.

(end of 1994, after visiting besieged Sarajevo)

Brothers

– Who's there? – Me. – Who are you?
– Don't you know me? Your brother.
– That's not you. I can't open the door.
Your voice makes me shudder.

– My voice is hoarse because of a storm.
I have trudged through snow and cold.
– Your eyes are full of wrath,
and your face looks very old.

– I am running from great terror.
Once you've seen blood flowing,
your eyes get bloodshot, glowing
with the fear of dying.

– You're a shadow of yourself,
my brother. What are you talking about?
– Someone came to my door, Death's scout,
the way I came to yours,

and said: Your dogs are poisoned.
No longer is your little boy alive.
Dead are your mother, daughter, wife.
I have killed them. For you to remember.

For you're no longer you. You're me.
Damned forever, you will bear my face

as long as lives the human race.
At the end of my eternal wandering,

my brother, I have found my way
to your door. Look, your son is alive
no longer. Nor your mother, daughter, wife.
I have killed them. For you to remember.

All your blood is poisoned.
You're no longer you, my brother.
All you still are is me, Defeat.
Damned forever, you will bear my face
as long as lives the human race.

TRANSLATED BY EVALD FLISAR

Springtime

In the Art Institute of Chicago
a Claude Monet hangs,
Torrent, Creuse,
a winter landscape with an oak tree.
To capture the frozen trembling
of the oaken forms
the painter hung so long on the canvas
that the oak tree began to turn green,
for spring had come in the land.
Desperate at the thought of losing the image
of an oak tree in winter,
Monet hired workers
to peel the young green foliage off
the oak day after day,
so as to keep it winterly at any cost,
naked, dead,
painterly alive.

Poetry is different.
For a long time I felt winter
inside and around me,
now that I want to write a winter poem
the poem is turning green,
for spring has come in the land,
and I don't have workers
to peel the greening
words off the reborn tree of a poem.
And even if I had an army of good, skillful elves,
the poem would not yield,

for words sprout up
whenever they do and however they do,
and there is nothing anyone can do about it.

That's why I eagerly, vernally, hasten my step
for I well know:
when summer comes in the land,
and autumn, and the next winter,
nothing will ever bring back
this painfully luxuriant
awakening in spring.
Nothing can ever bring anything back again.
O, the unwritten poems!
O, things forever lost!

I hasten, hasten my step
and with every word,
with every leaf
winter is getting nearer.

TRANSLATED BY MIA DINTINJANA

Keeping Awake

I wake over the deep whiteness of the paper,
I wake over the whiteness of unfolded sheets,
I wake over the spread dream where the bread
is getting stale and the last supper draws nearer,

I wake over the child and his dreaming mother,
like sailors through the night we hold each other
with both hands, while our steps are ticktacking
up and down the bedroom with no bottom,

but I am tired, I am so tired,
I wake over refugees pouring from the world's wound,
from the incurable abyss of the heart,
my head is getting heavy, and it will only get worse,

I wake over my absent self,
lost and dead, I am now someone else,
who still carries the body of my former
self, the body no longer fitting me,

I wake and wake, for I am the master of insomnia,
my only share of eternity,

I am tired to death, and it will only get worse.

TRANSLATED BY IRENA ZORKO

AND THE AUTHOR

Exile

No star can help me anymore.
I stare into the frozen northern skies,
the south is hidden. The white city
where I was raised lies
dying beyond the starry wall of the southern horizon.
An ever-thicker crust separates
me from myself. And I can only see
the shadow of my dead half through a moist
mist: as if I tremble, having no bottom,
and touch my dark face.
My only home is my throat.

TRANSLATED BY ANDREW WACHTEL

Letter

Mysteriously, more often do I think of you
in whom I do not believe. And yet, only
before you in silence does my knee
bend, ripping off the patches
of words and bleeding as in childhood.
You are familiar with the disheartened poverty
of all the hands that share a mortal fear of wounds.
Tell me, Jesus, did it hurt badly?
The lightning of pain tears the night and the palm.
Yet without the wound nothing remains whole.

You, who are not, follow me as a softness,
the first story's fear, the blue snow that wafts
from a dream, a cast-off sword at the bottom of a brook.
With light you shade the light soil of the grave
where I am smothered by evergreen boughs.
I am alone. I cannot cross the thirst
that forever divides our spines,
and yet I feel you close to me, like a shadow.
Tell me, Jesus, did it hurt badly?
Whatever is, or not is, hurts. Unbearably white.

You know what it is to be only for the others.
Not a whit for yourself. To watch your mother
weep alone upon the hill as you leave.
You could do it. You who are not.
Which is why I think of you now.
I cannot endure. Let the measure for my palm
be human, from dawn till dusk.

For the palm is a letter. Meant for touch. For children.
Tell me, Jesus, did it hurt badly?
If I were there, I would take your bleeding hand
in mine. It would make you feel better.

TRANSLATED BY MIA DINTINJANA

Father

As long as they live, parents stand
with their own bodies between death and us,
their children: destiny appears as if through a curtain.

I was hurt by your thin arms
when you died, o my only father:
still yours, but already foreign, too deep

they fell where I could not reach them,
into the air, yet quite near, here, to the spring
of tears, where I fall upon my face and weep.

In that terrible evening
when we washed the withered body
to return sweet unrest to the all-embracing peace,

I took upon myself, crystal-clear and amazed,
my own human death: since then I
am the father, I am the naked wound desperately

protecting the child against the hailstones
with the death of my own body
that grows from memory into the future

and sings, the rhythm of dance, the snow of farewell.
I fly across to the other side, bound by the law of the flock
of migratory birds, and I cry when I return to you,

my father.

(on the third anniversary of his death,
December 30th, 1994)

TRANSLATED BY MIA DINTINJANA

Intérieur

Mysterious are the characters of things close to us:
familiar as a man's face, yet strangely near
from ceaseless use: but between the two
who is a man and who is a garment?

Silent is the tongue of the shoes put on.
(Things that serve are silent.)
When I take them off, they suddenly speak up:
a bottomless abyss since I am no longer there.

When I put down my glasses, what do they see?
Without them I see only myself. Insane.
Things live, I am alive and alone.

I sleep alone in a closet. When I unlock my eyelids,
I see the gaping sleeves of my jacket
and my trousers without my legs. Empty.

TRANSLATED BY ERICA JOHNSON DEBELJAK

Rapid Disintegration

The rapidity of the world's disintegration is frightful.
It is more rapid than the disintegration of the body
into clay, clay into dust, dust into breath.
It is more rapid than the disintegration of the word
into a voice, a voice into a trace, a trace into ice.

The voice is the rapid disintegration of the word.
Time is the rapid disintegration of the body.
I am the rapid disintegration of the world.

TRANSLATED BY ERICA JOHNSON DEBELJAK

ALBA (1999)

Alba

Beyond the reach of sleepy dawn
in an unmade bed of half-light, fearful
of morning coming down from white mountains
between us with a sword that will not wait,

we lie, one against the other, still warm,
making a poor pretense of sleep,
while my palm, ever more breathlessly,
seeks to hold the willingness of the skin,

that melts beneath a starry touch.
Every instant takes you farther into the distance.
All that remains with me is your hidden picture.

Through the long but all too short night,
your warm head lies upon my shoulders.
And I hide my tears, my miraculous vulnerability.

TRANSLATED BY ERICA JOHNSON DEBELJAK

Borders

We gaze at the same full moon . . . horizons
far away, too far from each other. Mountains
rise between us. A soft, mossy crust
grows over our footsteps. All alone

you crossed all borders and came to a foreign country,
to the homeland of my arms. Dangerously alone
I crawl past the keepers of borders: I travel to the
northwest, where I am bitterly ashamed

of the screeching of the soul among smooth, horrible walls.
I stand before them, a dark man from the southeast,
with a conspicuous name, shuddering, as naked as prey.
I cannot escape. Border is destiny.

Now you know: although you cross the border, you don't erase it.
Rising even higher it will measure your steps, like doubt.
A map is not an illusion. So speak more softly.
Beyond all borders your lips are my home.

TRANSLATED BY LILI POTPARA

Your Little Bottles

I like to be with you in the bathroom.
Hundreds of scented bottles smile down
from the shelves: creams, lipsticks, shampoos,
mysterious little bottles that hold the condensed

memory of flowers with names unknown.
You borrow their aroma. In the evenings,
your soft breasts exhale their fragrance
and I rinse away the scent from the flowery

bottles with my lips. Then you paint yourself
anew. You make yourself beautiful for me
again: you blacken your brows so they are like birds

flying above the lakes of your eyes; you redden
your full lips so they are even more full, more perfect . . .
I know that women like to be alone at the hour

of their mysterious ablutions. But
I am your only witness. I enjoy watching you.

TRANSLATED BY ERICA JOHNSON DEBELJAK

Your Scent

Your scent wells up from the opulence of milk.
Your scent is milky mild and fresh and thick.
It washes over me like waves from distant rivers,
unseen air, the secrets of soothsayers.

You are dressed in it. Your scent is a robe
that never falls from you. A forest so thick
that even time cannot cut through it. Your scent
connects me to you: it is a delicate bridge.

When your own scent is concealed by the smell of flowers,
fragile and rich, I strip them away from you with tender
embraces. I lie inside of you: final and eternal.

The aroma of two bodies is a measure of happiness . . .
That is why I don't wash myself and your scent
steals furtively inside of me, mysterious and enduring,

timeless and placeless, stinging me.
I recognize your beauty and your unseen
trace as the most fatal of all words.
How far away you are. It is all in vain.

TRANSLATED BY ERICA JOHNSON DEBELJAK

Orpheus and Eurydice, Gare du Nord

And the train station
spreads the smell of distance.
The scent of you remains, burning
inside of me with the force of lava.
I must not move my head,
my senses are cursed.
I must not change the wager
and look at you as you go.

The myth of Orpheus is deceptive.
No serpent stung you in the high grass.
You are not leaving this place forever.
An ancient poem is not touching the true
color of your hair. I must not bring
a desert to life in a concrete basement
and look at you as you go.

The whole world leaves, the whole world
stays in a night of neon candles.
Timeless and placeless,
I see a repetition of pictures:
blue rooms, white sheets and coffee,
nakedness under the planets.
I must not move my head
and look at you as you go.

I must not look into that distance

that has mortally captured
your hips. I must not weep.
I must not move my head
and look at you as you go.

TRANSLATED BY ERICA JOHNSON DEBELJAK

ECHO (2000)

Living Shadow

Shadowy ancestor, I seek you everywhere.
I follow you where light still glows.
But I lose myself, for I am the heir
to your eternally obliterated grave.
Mine is a dim and late epoch:
the mirror, a vanishing well.
But you faithfully accompany me,
you are my living shadow.

I cannot follow you there. The anguish
of the past and the weight of the wreath
are more than I can bear. But a softness
remains, a miraculous presence.
I breathe the flowers from your grave.
I have been relieved of my shadow.

TRANSLATED BY ERICA JOHNSON DEBELJAK

Horse, Rider, Lake

I stroll around the lake
where light constantly shifts,
depending on the clouds. Crimson-blue,
a totally unreal hue, which from the snows

of nearby mountains floats like a haze
above the forest, touches my
heart, and all—water, the canopy of the sky,
memory—transforms into a letter, the air, the distance . . .

Here I often carried my son on the shoulders,
I was a horse and held in the stirrups
of my palms his wee little feet

and the rider called me with a thousand names . . .
All remains the same: road, forest, shore . . .
I am oppressed by the weight of bare, burden-free shoulders.

TRANSLATED BY MIA DINTINJANA

Confession

Who am I?

A traveler. Away from everything I love,
I travel far, to the end of the world, to an unseen
horizon where I am safely alone: to foreign lands.
My heart is deadly curious. There is nothing
left here. Everything has been erased. There is only
the vertiginous emptiness: the permanently
frozen beloved faces, the remembered hailstone
of touches, painfully present.

Who am I? A killer.

I behave systematically, cruelly, and radically.
From an incomprehensible, inner necessity.
I flee from all that is known and regular.
Foreign lands sweep over me.
From my birthplace, I have only the wealth
of words: the knife that cuts the sharpest.
Now I write a shameful, lonely letter to all
of you who I love and who I kill, that we are no more.

Who am I? A killer. I kill with my absence.

TRANSLATED BY ERICA JOHNSON DEBELJAK

Perpendicular Land

There is no room here: a field spreads
up, and a steep road leads downward.
Brooks stream like rain. All cities
rise to the sky. The only measure

of geometry is Height. People do not
walk on the ground but up the wall.
They carry one another on shoulders.
The only freedom is free fall. Whoever goes out

for a stroll, climbs: through chimney to the stars
and through basement back to the subconscious.
The heart, which knows no breadth, claws

deep into itself. The throat, nevertheless, draws
out a voice, shiveringly pure and blue,
made of immeasurable, unseen distances . . .

TRANSLATED BY MIA DINTINJANA

GLOWING (2003)

Discovering the Everyday
(vanishing sonnet)

I have never had a talent for life. For practical life,
that is. But since we have been together, I have been seized
by everydayness, by the miraculous spinning of hours,
days and nights, by the transformation of despair

into the patience of ceaseless ritual.
I go to buy a bed—wide enough for three—
because we will make love in it. I look
at the display of shirts and shoes, because you

are so beautifully dressed, that I must be too.
I discover the mysteries of washing and ironing.
Clean laundry has the softest complexion.

The greatest triumph is the preparation of lunch! . . .
I resist everydayness governed as it is by the strict
spirit of necessity. But each day is fathomless . . .

The until now unknown touch of things
permeates the frail skin of man. This universe

is woman . . .
I am learning to speak specifically:

not of birds, but of swallows and robins,

not of flowers, but carnations and roses . . .

TRANSLATED BY ERICA JOHNSON DEBELJAK

Our Supper

The preparation of food is an erotic matter.
I realize I am no cook, but I like to spin
around you, when you cook for us at the end
of the day. The smoke rises from the pot,

you slice the onions and soften them
in the pan, you marinate medallions of lamb
with spices—basil and mint, a hint of
Provençal herbs . . . For me, a small moment

of happiness is when I help to peel the potatoes
and—now with mastery—open a bottle of
red velvet, while you, with a spoon, conjure

mayonnaise out of nothing . . . A moth leads a dance
though the garden of candles where we eat.
Each bite is a kiss: prepared only for us and

consumed in this safe and hidden place,
as evening grows heavy above the rooftops . . .

A meal for two is an erotic matter,
especially in our unnamed place

where, after supper, we eagerly rush

to enjoy the fresh mellow fruit of our bodies . . .

TRANSLATED BY ERICA JOHNSON DEBELJAK

Our One House

We lie, after love, on a wrinkled
bed, intoxicated with the smell
of nearness yet already breathing
distance, and we sketch on the last page

of a scribbled notebook: a wide garden,
a big kitchen, dining alcove, and a room
flooded from a high window with the light
needed to write. Walls rise up from the

awkward letters, the colors will be bright,
in the bedroom a magnificent double bed,
the same one where we lie now

awake and dreaming and knowing—each
of us knowing but neither of us saying it aloud—
that this will be our one and only home,

our one safe and warm hiding place
in a jealous and lethal world,

this bed, this raft floating through time,
through the unfulfilled light of days . . .

Enough for love. Enough for death.

Too little for life . . .

TRANSLATED BY ERICA JOHNSON DEBELJAK

Birthday

Tomorrow will be a cut in time: my birthday.
I will have completed a well rounded fifty years.
The glasses will be full. The world will be full.
I will slip away for a moment

to give you a bouquet. I will sprinkle
kisses on your hand, wrinkled from the passage
of years. I am ashamed of my delusions
and forgetfulness. Let me now, when all is in vain,

embrace the dark, foundational memory.
Because my birthday is in truth yours.
Because on that day you were alone with yourself.

And then we were two. Alone together. Just the two of us.
From the depths of a dark and warm world,
your pain threw me into a painful magnet

of light, the human world, to which I have been condemned
for fifty years now. But then, standing in front of that cosmic door,

we were alone. Terribly alone. Mortally alone.
Just the two of us. I, your firstborn son,

and you, the first woman of my life,

my mother.

TRANSLATED BY ERICA JOHNSON DEBELJAK

Timelessness

Summer, timeless, without measure:
on the surface of the sea, shimmering orbs
of glowing light, the serene evening primordial
sun sinking into night, behind a charcoal

horizon already scattered with stars,
the shore where you take my hand,
a reflection of warm waves splashing, foam
the dowry at a wedding of waves and reefs,

and it's fine to be with you, the days are salty,
the evenings sweet, on the wide veranda
of the coffee house, the sea in my palms,

the best ice cream in the world
never melts, the timeless taste of
the seashore for which I no longer have words,

and of which you have no memory, but which
is awakened by the taste of the ice cream

that you eat alone on the little terrace of room
2C, you listen to the wind in the pines and

the hum of the highway on the other side, where lonely

children rush by who have no time, good-bye, good-bye . . .

TRANSLATED BY ERICA JOHNSON DEBELJAK

Give Us Each Day Our Daily Death

In the old house where Fate was at home
—a home that is no more since a suburban
highway cut like a ruler through the valley—
there stands the bed that held the cries of birth

and also the cries of death . . . *Give us each day
our daily death* . . . On the evening before a birth,
the midwife put aside the most beautiful sheets
to serve, just in case, as death's shroud.

The old woman with the scythe, a picture in an old calendar.
She lifted the scythe above your head: when you walked
barefoot, when on the dewy flowers you tread . . .

The old tires of our new masters are there.
And the old bed. And the old scythe.
And the old age of calendars. Slowly decaying . . .

Time passes quickly. The patients on the veranda
stare into emptiness, and Death wears

a doctor's robe, white as an apparition.
He comes and goes quietly.

Through the wall.

Forever closed.

TRANSLATED BY ERICA JOHNSON DEBELJAK

Death in the Feet

Death always begins its task
in the feet. The toes are the first to go.
The soles grow cold, the chill of flesh
up to the knee, the skin an unnatural white.

The step slows and the sense of balance
weakens. As if death is hacking away
at invisible roots. Time staggers and your heels
no longer anchor you to the ground.

Death will advance. Like ice in the roof gutters,
extending its grip across your tired belly,
that rose up three times to the sky

with the birth of three miracles, the miracle of birth...
But that will not be enough, because for death
there is never enough. Death will not be restrained.

Behold, death rises like a moist powder
up the unprotected walls. It will be triumphant.

It will climb up to your shoulder, to your mouth,
and your eyes. But, mother, don't give up!

Walk, march, trample upon it! Trample fear!

Trample death under your feet!

TRANSLATED BY ERICA JOHNSON DEBELJAK

From Beginning to End

Da Capo al Fine

You hold my hand when we go for a walk,
and the sun goes with us, the trees in the park,
the leaves awakening with each shaft of light
the life around you soft and bright,

life smiles, bids farewell to winter,
two sparrows fly to the other side of the tracks,
I escape from your hand and run after them,
everything I remember is a small part of those long

seconds when your tore me away from death,
from the frightening dragon-shape of the tramway . . .
Oh, let that moment happen again and again:

I hold your hand when we go for a walk,
and the sun goes with us, the trees in the park,
the leaves awakening with each shaft of light

the life around you soft and bright,
life smiles, bids farewell to winter,

I hold you with the desperation of a grown-up son,
so you won't slip from my fingers, mother, to a place

far from me, far from yourself, a place where I have

no strength, there on the sunless side of memory . . .

TRANSLATED BY ERICA JOHNSON DEBELJAK

Soul

Stranger, with that kiss you opened up a mystery in me,
your whole presence melting away under my mouth. Ljubljana
in December, the rush to shop, the holiday whiteness. You took
the number six bus to the market from Črnuče through Dolgi
  Most.

In the crowded bus, I catch a fleeting glance of a hat leaning
  oddly
against the glass. The gentleman is tired, I think. Sleeping in his
  seat.
The basket in his hand falls to the floor and his hat as well.
And then a vertiginous moment. I kneel down, lean over

your still warm body, and fill the emptiness of your lungs
with desperate artificial breaths. That kiss gave me the key:
I knew everything about you. You were a gentleman. You laid the
  foundations.

Suffered inside. Now hair of snow and dentures in your mouth.
  Clean.
When I take them out, your face darkens to dust, moss, withered
  leaves.
Oh soul, I am the last person to meet you on the face of this
  earth.

TRANSLATED BY ERICA JOHNSON DEBELJAK

The Hairclip

You are a prophetess, Ariadne, in the story's labyrinth:
all day you search for the thread behind the plinth.
After sweet hours of love, golden slumber
vanquishes your weary head. Feather light

curls fall upon your brow. The first shadow
sends a faint trace across your heavy lids.
Your skin, the color of milk, softly breathes.
The murmur of your blood finds its slow reprieve.

And now you ask me to take the clip
from your plaited hair. Your sleepy voice
sounds girlish. Moved by this sign of intimacy,

I carefully unlatch the hairclip so as not to prick you.
Your hair pours out over the pillowcase. Stay
that way. I lie beside you, humbled by the silence.

TRANSLATED BY ERICA JOHNSON DEBELJAK

Magic Suitcase

A month after returning from my travels,
the suitcase still lingers by my bed.
I should put it away in the cellar,
but cannot, because it contains

memories of the warm, short, airy days
by your side. This suitcase of mine is a vagabond,
divided between here and there. A wanderer,
floating among the dark stars, a Jew longing for . . .

This suitcase holds a mere twenty kilos but is,
in fact, a magic treasure chest where miracles
are stored: the scent of your skirts, the softness

of our bed, the view on to the cathedral
from the window of our attic room,
the sound of the bell and its silent echo,

the memory of your hand sleeping on my chest
and the moon unraveling its silver skein

through the ancient streets and market squares,
the tangled branches of our bodies . . .

After some time, I steel my resolve: away suitcase! Away to the cold
    cellar,

far from my eyes! I must make order. I breathe through gills . . .

TRANSLATED BY ERICA JOHNSON DEBELJAK

Intimate Things

My suitcase is at your place, your traveling bag
at mine. Chaos. You find my socks in the laundry
basket. Your nightgown is my eternal hostage:
it smells of fresh soap . . .

I often look for a shirt or a pair of pants,
in vain, because they are with you, twelve hundred
kilometers away. I'd like to live life differently,
to focus the world in only one place,

but it doesn't work: the world is too large. We share
a temporary roof, each with our own suitcase,
reaching out for a new place. Nights are together, days divided . . .

If we part from each other, let our things
remain as they are, let them turn to
stone:
    mine at your place,
             and yours at mine . . .

TRANSLATED BY ERICA JOHNSON DEBELJAK

Decisions: 11

Between two words
choose the quieter one.

Between word and silence
choose listening.

Between two books
choose the dustier one.

Between the earth and the sky
choose a bird.

Between two animals
choose the one who needs you more.

Between two children
choose both.

Between the lesser and the bigger evil
choose neither.

Between hope and despair
choose hope:
it will be harder to bear.

TRANSLATED BY MIA DINTINJANA

My Doppelganger

I have a doppelganger. While I,
vain as I am, show myself to the world,
he sits at home and works, works, works . . .
My faithful slave, my face known to no one.

I chain him to a cold radiator
and pour him a glass of water
(so he won't die of thirst). I owe him
the light of my freedom, he, my gladiator.

He eats little, is grateful for a bit of dry bread and a dark hello.
He sleeps little, only a few hours each night.
When I stagger in exhaustion, he rushes to my aid.

He is the one who writes; I only put my signature there.
Now he's blushing in embarrassment. My intimate stranger,
my doppelganger. I wish I knew him a little better.

TRANSLATED BY ERICA JOHNSON DEBELJAK

To the Poet I Was

I was fifteen years old. I became a poet
on the first of September, the year nineteen
sixty-nine. It was a blow beneath my ribs,
and I floated above the earth, magus, magus, magnet

of mystery! I burned, my gaze illuminated things
with its smile: everything shone with my elation!
In front of my parents, I pretended to be an ordinary boy,
but actually I was a thousand years old. I liked to stand

at the window and watch the reflection of street lights
in the puddles: I SAW the glowing sign of the miraculous,
the immeasurable value of this world.

Strange: I felt no need to write poems.
To prove I was a poet with words—
how banal! . . . Today when I look at streetlights

and puddles, I see only things. Lights. Puddles. Stones.
Today I write poems with words. But the poet,

the poet I was then, when I floated above the earth . . .

TRANSLATED BY ERICA JOHNSON DEBELJAK

LPM: LITTLE PERSONAL MYTHOLOGY (2007)

My Grandfather Anton Novak, *Tausendkünstler*

My grandfather was a jack-of-all-trades, a tinker
of the greatest magnitude, a renovator of ideas,
and a fearless spirit. Above the shanks of his mustaches,
sprouted a nose that was always and ever thrust forward.

In France, such a *bricoleur* would be a mensch, a wise guy,
an academic with some money in his pocket and a Nobel Prize.
This *Murskler*, this Einstein of Maribor, gave away God's
gift in exchange for a modest, narrow, difficult survival.

He was *Tausendkünstler*: a hunter of poisonous snakes, a supplier
of decorative starfish and sea urchins for the market nets,
a producer of notes for the zither, the genial inventor

of the "*Novak method*" for the conservation of butterflies
in boxes that can still be seen now mysteriously fresh
in the Zagreb Museum of Natural History with their wings

curled up and their markings like precious gems.
He was a charming smuggler carrying his violin across all borders

and a gambler who salvaged the family budget
at the gaming tables again and again and again.

It is from you, my grandfather, that I inherited my talent for air:

I invent forms and hunt for butterfly words.

TRANSLATED BY ERICA JOHNSON DEBELJAK

Turtles

My mad grandfather was not only an entrepreneur—
but he was a champion in the art of raising children,
an unsurpassed artist, a master-of-all-trades.
He could do anything!

He always kept twenty turtles at home.
For sale. —His six-year old son, my father,
had to perform the impossible each day:
he had to take a herd of twenty turtles to a nearby

park to graze. The turtles stared at him with their turtle
eyes: he was their pastor, their food, air, and water,
and he was able to provide them with the peak of turtle delight—

lettuce! But more than lettuces, the turtles loved
their freedom as did we. My father ran from one to the other
so they wouldn't get away. The children liked to play

with the turtles and sometimes even stole one or two,
which is why he asked a sweet little neighborhood girl

to help him watch over his exotic herd . . .
It would be hard to find a more beautiful word

for one's father: he was

a pastor of turtles.

TRANSLATED BY ERICA JOHNSON DEBELJAK

The Secret of Life

This poem is about a safe that held the secret of life.
It excited me greatly when I was little. It squatted
there in Aunt Mara's sitting room, copper brown,
as silent as the Sphinx. Opinions abounded

but no one knew for certain what was inside.
Herr Holzer, solicitor and amateur photographer,
asked Mr. Novak to watch over it during the Maister
Uprising. Until "*diese Scheisse*" has passed, he said,

he would return for it then. Until that time, Mr. Novak
would be its guard. But Herr Holzer never came back.
Not then or later. Countries rose and fell. Borders changed.
When money ran low, someone always recommended

that the safe be opened. Out of necessity.
Mr. Novak said no and no: "I am a man of my word!
True, I am as poor as a church mouse, but no misery
will make me steal what is not mine."

We children imagined that the safe was ours.
That a pirate's treasure was hidden inside.
The closed safe attracted us like a vertiginous abyss,
a cosmic black hole, passion and fear, mystery and lust! . . .

In the year 1982, after the death of Aunt Mara,
the *state safebreaker* finally jimmied the rusted lock,
but no gold, no treasure, was hidden in that black hole! . . .
. . . only diaries and photograph albums and old

envelopes. —Diaries on top: in which Herr Holzer
described in detail his trysts with an enviable
number of beautiful women from high society . . .
Their dark mounds of Venus on a background of white linen

shone brightly from the photographs, all those refined
and naked women preserved forever like the unending lust
of the human heart . . . And, at the bottom of the safe,
a pile of envelopes, each one filled with hair from down there!

Differently curled—different colors—women's pubic hair!
Oh, tender souvenirs! And on each envelope, a woman's name
Was written in Gothic letters of red ink. Time had not erased them
because Mr. Novak had so loyally protected Herr Holzer's secret . . .

The moral of this poem is simple and instructive:
the mystery of life is not gold or the key to a safe-deposit box
but———

TRANSLATED BY ERICA JOHNSON DEBELJAK

Ragology (The Study of Rags)

All her life, our *nona* waged
a systematic battle against dust,
mud, and all manner of filth and muss.
To this end, she developed a precise strategy,
the study of rags, known to her family as *ragology*
At any moment, she would have arrayed
before her some seventeen different rags
that she would send into combat
as division generals in the battle field.
God forbid any unauthorized use
of one or the other for the wrong purpose!
Whoever did so received
the strictest of punishments.
In this regard, our *nona* did not trust even her maid,
and followed her movements with the sharpest gaze.
In the end, she preferred to dispatch her army of rags herself
with her own feet and hands.
I shall enumerate the various types of rags and cloths
using the scientific terminology of *nona*'s ragology:

1) the "rough" one for the stairs to the front door;
2) the "fine" one for the marble in the *entrée*;
3) the "soft" one for waxing the old parquet;
4) the "plush" one made from pieces of old clothing
    for the copper tiles under the hearth;
5) the "big" absorbent one for the stone floor on the terrace;
6) the "little" absorbent one for the stone floor in the kitchen
    and the bathroom;

7) the "old" clean one for the pots and other metal pans;

8) the "new" clean one for the porcelain service;

9) the "sensitive" one for the wine glasses;

10) the "fast" one for the knives;

11) the "clever" one for the forks;

12) the "pedantic" one for the spoons;

13) the "shiny" one for the silver;

14) the "splendid" one for the mirror;

15) the "see-through" rag for the ironing;

16) the "male" rag for the military boots;

17) the "chic" rag for her own high-heeled shoes.

Nona's explanation for these all-important ragological distinctions
was passionately detailed and deeply considered
—knives were smooth and generally not put in the mouth
hence a simple treatment with the "quick" rag would suffice;
—little scraps of food tended to get lodged between the tines
of the fork, hence the need for careful treatment with the "clever"
    rag;
spoons that we like to lick so much and which relentlessly attract
a great number of bacteria, require serious
and radical hygienic measures that can only
be assured by the "pedantic" rag.

But all this advanced and specialized study of rags,
all of these seventeen fanatical divisions of the anti-dust armada,
sent day and night into pitched battle
against the great filth of the world,
regularly deployed and redeployed,
all this bourgeois order,

that represented meaning and purpose in her life,
could not help,
could not prevent,
our *nona*,
our own dear *nona*,
our own dear *nona*'s life from falling apart,
            from being scattered about,
                  irretrievably dispersed
like so much ash and dust.

TRANSLATED BY ERICA JOHNSON DEBELJAK

One Poem about Three People and Two Coats

It was a great and beautiful love. When they parted—it was
    winter,
winter outside, winter inside, they were in the grip of ice—
he saw that Milena was cold. She didn't have a coat.
He took his off and wrapped it round her beloved shoulders . . .

When my father saw that his brother Leo was cold
because he had no coat, he took his own off and gave it to
    him . . .
Mysterious is the fate of coats. We wear them out of need,
and the coats wear our stories . . . When my father stood

coatless on the threshold of that first post-war winter, he
    shivered.
At the secondhand shop, they offered him a coat for a man of small
    stature.
It fit him like a glove. Strangely familiar. Then he found a secret
    pocket!

His secret pocket! It was his old coat, the one he'd given Leo!
The one Leo no longer needed. The coat had been a warm, living
    armor.
Leo had left without a coat, naked and barefoot. In a winter that
    burned . . .

In her old age, the actress Milena Godina wrote to me
that an old coat, given to her by her fiancée, my uncle Leo

had kept her warm her whole life. One coat is always missing.
Someone must always leave, shivering, a dreadful winter in the
body.

And someone always remains wrapped in a coat of kisses and
memories,

in a coat of fragrance and touch, alone in loss . . .

TRANSLATED BY ERICA JOHNSON DEBELJAK

Butterflies

Just one week before his death, Mr. Novak took his net
and—like the morning before—went out to catch butterflies.
He was accompanied by the neighbor boy, small, lively, and
    gentle.
The old man taught him how to place the fragile things

into a special case and how to hold their wings
so the fingers wouldn't damage that trace of dust,
without which they couldn't fly, these tender,
fluttering, colorful hearts at the bottom

of the sky . . . At the tragicomic funeral
of this incurable atheist, the cross removed
from his coffin, all the mourners wearing

their coats inside out, seams exposed,
the boy opened a box full of butterflies
and they took sudden flight to the sky,

so fluttering, tender, and mild, so wonderfully alive!
Oh, the ascension of colors! A swarm of flying hearts!

A butterfly flew into the eulogizer's throat.
He stood by the open grave. The whole world stood.

The sky opened.

And God smiled.

TRANSLATED BY ERICA JOHNSON DEBELJAK

The Image of a Partisan

In one of the few photographs of a partisan
—for reasons of safety they shunned them—
he smiles, as if he has forgotten for a moment
his role of commandant. A half-smoked

cigarette dangles from the corner
of his mouth. A rough cap sits aslant
on his head. He is the image
of a rebel standing vulnerable

and naked before death, deeming it trivial.
The image is slightly blurred, the eyes
both steely gray and gentle . . .

An eternal moment of calm,
though his muscles, quivering with tension,
could hardly carry such a terribly heavy load.

He saw too much, experienced too much, died too many
times, and survived this deadly world too many times.

This loyal soldier of history, an old man
before his time, smiling despite the onslaught,

the tears, the death, and the madness—

that is the image of my father's youth.

TRANSLATED BY ERICA JOHNSON DEBELJAK

The First and Last Home

These days you mostly lie about, exhausted.
You can no longer walk. Your still lovely face,
Mother, ceaselessly, oddly changes expression:
as if your cheeks are being trimmed by a strange blast

of powerful wind, stronger than the immobility
of your withered body, once so womanly.
This dreaded farewell is full of the quotidian,
even more so the dreaded certainty . . .

When I kiss your hair, I still detect
the smell of years both near and distant,
all time mysteriously the same, cursed,

like the day before yesterday, like yesterday,
when you kissed me goodnight
and I smelled the scent of your hair,

an aroma I can't describe with words,
the voice of silence, my earliest memory,

the loveliest and most familiar scent,
to which, I, the grown-up boy, returns.

It will soon dissipate into the air and I

will remain, bereft of my first and last home

TRANSLATED BY ERICA JOHNSON DEBELJAK

Jealous Pajamas

No garment absorbs
scents as deeply as pajamas,
a second nocturnal skin shimmering
through the night, awake, alone, above

the dreams and nightmares of the sweating
body that makes wrinkles in the cloth.
Morning memories of the horizontal
dance of limbs, the press of kisses

on naked skin, while the pajamas,
pushed to the side, jealously frown,
embarrassed by the images of naked flesh:

pajamas are like a refined old lady . . .
When their owner dresses and walks away
into the noisy day, they doze for an hour or so.

Then, all wrinkled, wake again, silently
dreaming, and waiting, waiting, waiting . . .

But, indeed, my pajamas like it most
when you put them on: they're much too big for you.

They billow around your legs and titillate me

with your scent, sweet, sweeter, and sweetest of all . . .

TRANSLATED BY ERICA JOHNSON DEBELJAK

FRAGMENTS FROM THE EPOS (2009–12)

Tidying up after the Dead

Even now, as I write this, the taste of ash
fills my mouth and it is hard to breathe. Because
tidying up after the dead is a horror. To pass

a whole life through a sieve, to choose among
the unfortunate things destined for the hell of oblivion,
and the more happy ones, for the paradise of memory.

To find in this legacy gold used for fillings
and for wedding rings, bracelets, and pocket
watches with broken hands, the old detritus

of souvenirs and letters, visiting cards and
postcards, important documents and photographs,
a sewing kit, a box of buttons, a broken necklace

and rusted keys, fruit rotting in the refrigerator,
someone's first tooth, primary-school textbooks,
a dozen glasses with different lenses and frames,

two dozen identification cards and passports,
paintings and prints, and shelves filled to overflowing
with dusty books, books, books, books . . .

A last glance at a life, amazement, what a beauty
my mother was when she was young, the scent
in her skirts, her rounded soul hovering in the pleats,

so lovely. —My memory of her will live until her scent
abandons the empty clothes. —Tidying up after the dead
is a bittersweet ritual that revives for the last time

everything that she once was and had, before the death
shroud erased all traces. It's a terrible dilemma,
what to keep and what to throw away. Discarded

memories roam in boxes closed forever.
Two evening dresses with matching silk scarves,
which pair should I save from oblivion? . . .

The zeal of the living continues relentlessly, the force
of the present pushing aside the weight of the past.
All those closets filled with junk would suffocate us,

we must make room, cleanse our memory,
lest it collapse under the weight of the burning
cargo it carries . . .
            It burns for so long,

that statuette from the Horn of Africa—
who brought it so far, to this Alpine land—
and a faded letter, a passionate appeal,

from my father to my mother, just before they

became father and mother, dated 1953, *April 9*,
that father wanted to destroy but mother saved

after his death for future eyes, and now
I also save because I, who my mother—so feminine,
so mild—carried then, am mentioned in it.

I am tormented by the question: what will be the fate
of this letter when my time comes—the next tidying-up
by the living of the traces left behind by the dead?
                    Will another face

lean over this letter and dream of lives lived
and lives ended? Will my parents' love be tossed
in the garbage bin
            or in the box of memory?

Silence descends . . .

TRANSLATED BY ERICA JOHNSON DEBELJAK

A Final Account

I don't know why as a child I eavesdropped
on adult conversations. I lay on the floor
of my father's office and pretended to play

with Lego blocks, but really listened to the laughter
and the serious pronouncements of all those men,
those *uncles* as I called them. While putting the roofs

on the plastic houses, I searched for the echo of *truth*
in the deathly terrifying stories of heroism and crimes
from the war and after. I heard the word *injustice*

for the first time, and *torture*, *jail*, and *trial*,
the faces of fallen comrades shrouded
in the silent past emerged from the memories

of those who happened to survive, I heard them
whisper of *defeats* that could not be spoken of aloud,
of *betrayals* and *accusations* and *verdicts*, I heard

in these expressions the emotional charge of postwar times—
and although I understood nothing, their words were
recorded on the hard disk of my memory, an avalanche

of decades . . .
        The uncles were convinced I couldn't understand
the miseries and horrors because I was a child. But I know
the past from their words. What did I discover? . . .

The red and white blocks grew into houses, the room
filled with smoke, the uncles praised me, saying I would
be an excellent engineer one day. They had already left behind

the light of construction and the twilight of destruction,
and were flying toward the future on winds of Progress.
After the war, the world needed not soldiers, but for the ruins

to be rebuilt. And I, an engineer, already seven years of age,
was the sole assurance, for my father and all those uncles,
that time would move onward, that they would no longer be

trapped in the circle of revenge. But I didn't tell them the truth:
that I would not be an engineer or an architect, but instead—
Sherlock Holmes! I kissed my father on the cheek

and went to bed . . .
                    At the bottom of those distant years,
I can still sense the thick and acrid smell of tobacco,
still feel the smooth surface of the Lego blocks under my fingers,

and the allure of all those strange tales in the thickening
     twilight . . .
And as I knew then: I would not be an engineer or an architect,
but a detective! . . .
                    I have been waiting years and years now

for the key that will open the secret door, the cellar
of memory, clarify the logic of coincidence, so I may make
a sequence of events from all those unconnected fragments,

from two photographs taken in a weak light
I try to decipher them, who is *that* figure,
to find the thread in the scattered stories,

I compare the contradictory accounts of distant
times, I read the books of one-sided memories,
and I listen to the silence of the forgotten, but the real

image retreats, murky as the sediment
of blood, multiplied in a polished mirror,
scattering like sparks consumed by the darkness,

I have the feeling that I am missing only a tiny fragment,
that for years I've been searching for a solitary witness, a single
    sentence
that would break through all the intrigues in the background,

I wonder if it will remain unfinished, like a body without a head
and a head without eyes, I am putting together a *puzzle* that is
    missing
the essential piece, I overlooked it or lost it, I cannot find

the real image, who is *that* strange woman
in the old photograph, death or love,
embrace or a trap, all equations leave a remainder,

words are more reliable, the ones I heard
from my father and my uncles when I was an engineer,
words that I didn't understand at the time but that I remember

exactly . . .

I still don't understand. Maybe I will
never find the truth. Maybe the truth would be worse
than the worst nightmare. Maybe it doesn't exist . . .

It is what it is. I, who do not understand—
stranger to myself, investigator of my own heritage—
I must give a final account of my research . . .

Here it is.

TRANSLATED BY ERICA JOHNSON DEBELJAK

Born in Serbia (then Yugoslavia) in 1953, BORIS A. NOVAK is a poet, playwright, editor, essayist, and translator of Bosnian, British, American, French, Provençal, Italian, German, Dutch (Flemish), and Spanish poetry into Slovenian. He is considered one of the most important living Slovenian poets, and has seventeen books of poetry for adults, and eight books of poetry for children to his name. He is a Professor at the Department for Comparative Literature and Literary Theory in the Faculty of Arts at the University of Ljubljana.

In 2010, the Slovenian Book Agency took a bold step toward solving the problem of how few literary works are now translated into English, initiating a program to provide financial support for a series dedicated to Slovenian literature at Dalkey Archive Press. Partially evolving from a relationship that Dalkey Archive and the Vilenica International Literary Festival had developed a few years previously, this program will go on to ensure that both classic and contemporary works from Slovenian are brought into English, while allowing the Press to undertake marketing efforts far exceeding what publishers can normally provide for works in translation.

Slovenia has always held a great reverence for literature, with the Slovenian national identity being forged through its fiction and poetry long before the foundation of the contemporary Republic: "It is precisely literature that has in some profound, subtle sense safeguarded the Slovenian community from the imperialistic appetites of stronger and more expansive nations in the region," writes critic Andrej Inkret. Never insular, Slovenian writing has long been in dialogue with the great movements of world literature, from the romantic to the experimental, seeing the literary not as distinct from the world, but as an integral means of perceiving and even amending it.

Petros Abatzoglou, *What Does Mrs. Freeman Want?*
Michal Ajvaz, *The Golden Age.*
The Other City.
Pierre Albert-Birot, *Grabinoulor.*
Yuz Aleshkovsky, *Kangaroo.*
Felipe Alfau, *Chromos.*
Locos.
João Almino, *The Book of Emotions.*
Ivan Ângelo, *The Celebration.*
The Tower of Glass.
David Antin, *Talking.*
António Lobo Antunes, *Knowledge of Hell.*
The Splendor of Portugal.
Alain Arias-Misson, *Theatre of Incest.*
Iftikhar Arif and Waqas Khwaja, eds., *Modern Poetry of Pakistan.*
John Ashbery and James Schuyler, *A Nest of Ninnies.*
Robert Ashley, *Perfect Lives.*
Gabriela Avigur-Rotem, *Heatwave and Crazy Birds.*
Heimrad Bäcker, *transcript.*
Djuna Barnes, *Ladies Almanack.*
Ryder.
John Barth, *LETTERS.*
Sabbatical.
Donald Barthelme, *The King.*
Paradise.
Svetislav Basara, *Chinese Letter.*
Miquel Bauçà, *The Siege in the Room.*
René Belletto, *Dying.*
Marek Bieńczyk, *Transparency.*
Mark Binelli, *Sacco and Vanzetti Must Die!*
Andrei Bitov, *Pushkin House.*
Andrej Blatnik, *You Do Understand.*
Louis Paul Boon, *Chapel Road.*
My Little War.
Summer in Termuren.
Roger Boylan, *Killoyle.*
Ignácio de Loyola Brandão, *Anonymous Celebrity.*
The Good-Bye Angel.
Teeth under the Sun.
Zero.
Bonnie Bremser, *Troia: Mexican Memoirs.*
Christine Brooke-Rose, *Amalgamemnon.*
Brigid Brophy, *In Transit.*
Meredith Brosnan, *Mr. Dynamite.*
Gerald L. Bruns, *Modern Poetry and the Idea of Language.*
Evgeny Bunimovich and J. Kates, eds., *Contemporary Russian Poetry: An Anthology.*
Gabrielle Burton, *Heartbreak Hotel.*
Michel Butor, *Degrees.*
Mobile.
Portrait of the Artist as a Young Ape.
G. Cabrera Infante, *Infante's Inferno.*
Three Trapped Tigers.
Julieta Campos, *The Fear of Losing Eurydice.*
Anne Carson, *Eros the Bittersweet.*
Orly Castel-Bloom, *Dolly City.*
Camilo José Cela, *Christ versus Arizona.*
The Family of Pascual Duarte.
The Hive.
Louis-Ferdinand Céline, *Castle to Castle.*
Conversations with Professor Y.
London Bridge.
Normance.
North.
Rigadoon.
Marie Chaix, *The Laurels of Lake Constance.*
Hugo Charteris, *The Tide Is Right.*
Jerome Charyn, *The Tar Baby.*
Eric Chevillard, *Demolishing Nisard.*
Luis Chitarroni, *The No Variations.*
Marc Cholodenko, *Mordechai Schamz.*
Joshua Cohen, *Witz.*
Emily Holmes Coleman, *The Shutter of Snow.*
Robert Coover, *A Night at the Movies.*
Stanley Crawford, *Log of the S.S. The Mrs Unguentine.*
Some Instructions to My Wife.
Robert Creeley, *Collected Prose.*
René Crevel, *Putting My Foot in It.*
Ralph Cusack, *Cadenza.*
Susan Daitch, *L.C.*
Storytown.
Nicholas Delbanco, *The Count of Concord.*
Sherbrookes.
Nigel Dennis, *Cards of Identity.*
Peter Dimock, *A Short Rhetoric for Leaving the Family.*
Ariel Dorfman, *Konfidenz.*
Coleman Dowell, *The Houses of Children.*
Island People.
Too Much Flesh and Jabez.
Arkadii Dragomoshchenko, *Dust.*
Rikki Ducornet, *The Complete Butcher's Tales.*
The Fountains of Neptune.
The Jade Cabinet.
The One Marvelous Thing.
Phosphor in Dreamland.
The Stain.
The Word "Desire."
William Eastlake, *The Bamboo Bed.*
Castle Keep.
Lyric of the Circle Heart.
Jean Echenoz, *Chopin's Move.*
Stanley Elkin, *A Bad Man.*
Boswell: A Modern Comedy.
Criers and Kibitzers, Kibitzers and Criers.
The Dick Gibson Show.
The Franchiser.
George Mills.
The Living End.
The MacGuffin.
The Magic Kingdom.
Mrs. Ted Bliss.
The Rabbi of Lud.
Van Gogh's Room at Arles.
François Emmanuel, *Invitation to a Voyage.*
Annie Ernaux, *Cleaned Out.*
Salvador Espriu, *Ariadne in the Grotesque Labyrinth.*
Lauren Fairbanks, *Muzzle Thyself.*
Sister Carrie.
Leslie A. Fiedler, *Love and Death in the American Novel.*
Juan Filloy, *Faction.*
Op Oloop.
Andy Fitch, *Pop Poetics.*
Gustave Flaubert, *Bouvard and Pécuchet.*
Kass Fleisher, *Talking out of School.*

SELECTED DALKEY ARCHIVE TITLES

WALLACE MARKFIELD,
  Teitlebaum's Window.
  To an Early Grave.
DAVID MARKSON, *Reader's Block.*
  Springer's Progress.
  Wittgenstein's Mistress.
CAROLE MASO, *AVA.*
LADISLAV MATEJKA AND KRYSTYNA
  POMORSKA, EDS.,
  Readings in Russian Poetics:
    Formalist and Structuralist Views.
HARRY MATHEWS,
  The Case of the Persevering Maltese:
    Collected Essays.
  Cigarettes.
  The Conversions.
  The Human Country: New and
    Collected Stories.
  The Journalist.
  My Life in CIA.
  Singular Pleasures.
  The Sinking of the Odradek
    Stadium.
  Tlooth.
  20 Lines a Day.
JOSEPH MCELROY,
  Night Soul and Other Stories.
THOMAS MCGONIGLE,
  Going to Patchogue.
ROBERT L. MCLAUGHLIN, ED., *Innovations:*
    An Anthology of Modern &
    Contemporary Fiction.
ABDELWAHAB MEDDEB, *Talismano.*
GERHARD MEIER, *Isle of the Dead.*
HERMAN MELVILLE, *The Confidence-Man.*
AMANDA MICHALOPOULOU, *I'd Like.*
STEVEN MILLHAUSER, *The Barnum Museum.*
  In the Penny Arcade.
RALPH J. MILLS, JR., *Essays on Poetry.*
MOMUS, *The Book of Jokes.*
CHRISTINE MONTALBETTI, *The Origin of Man.*
  Western.
OLIVE MOORE, *Spleen.*
NICHOLAS MOSLEY, *Accident.*
  Assassins.
  Catastrophe Practice.
  Children of Darkness and Light.
  Experience and Religion.
  A Garden of Trees.
  God's Hazard.
  The Hesperides Tree.
  Hopeful Monsters.
  Imago Bird.
  Impossible Object.
  Inventing God.
  Judith.
  Look at the Dark.
  Natalie Natalia.
  Paradoxes of Peace.
  Serpent.
  Time at War.
  The Uses of Slime Mould:
    Essays of Four Decades.
WARREN MOTTE,
  Fables of the Novel: French Fiction
    since 1990.
  Fiction Now: The French Novel in
    the 21st Century.
  Oulipo: A Primer of Potential
    Literature.
GERALD MURNANE, *Barley Patch.*
  Inland.

YVES NAVARRE, *Our Share of Time.*
  Sweet Tooth.
DOROTHY NELSON, *In Night's City.*
  Tar and Feathers.
ESHKOL NEVO, *Homesick.*
WILFRIDO D. NOLLEDO, *But for the Lovers.*
FLANN O'BRIEN, *At Swim-Two-Birds.*
  At War.
  The Best of Myles.
  The Dalkey Archive.
  Further Cuttings.
  The Hard Life.
  The Poor Mouth.
  The Third Policeman.
CLAUDE OLLIER, *The Mise-en-Scène.*
  Wert and the Life Without End.
GIOVANNI ORELLI, *Walaschek's Dream.*
PATRIK OUŘEDNÍK, *Europeana.*
  The Opportune Moment, 1855.
BORIS PAHOR, *Necropolis.*
FERNANDO DEL PASO, *News from the Empire.*
  Palinuro of Mexico.
ROBERT PINGET, *The Inquisitory.*
  Mahu or The Material.
  Trio.
A. G. PORTA, *The No World Concerto.*
MANUEL PUIG, *Betrayed by Rita Hayworth.*
  The Buenos Aires Affair.
  Heartbreak Tango.
RAYMOND QUENEAU, *The Last Days.*
  Odile.
  Pierrot Mon Ami.
  Saint Glinglin.
ANN QUIN, *Berg.*
  Passages.
  Three.
  Tripticks.
ISHMAEL REED, *The Free-Lance Pallbearers.*
  The Last Days of Louisiana Red.
  Ishmael Reed: The Plays.
  Juice!
  Reckless Eyeballing.
  The Terrible Threes.
  The Terrible Twos.
  Yellow Back Radio Broke-Down.
JASIA REICHARDT, *15 Journeys Warsaw*
    to London.
NOËLLE REVAZ, *With the Animals.*
JOÃO UBALDO RIBEIRO, *House of the*
    Fortunate Buddhas.
JEAN RICARDOU, *Place Names.*
RAINER MARIA RILKE, *The Notebooks of*
    Malte Laurids Brigge.
JULIÁN RÍOS, *The House of Ulysses.*
  Larva: A Midsummer Night's Babel.
  Poundemonium.
  Procession of Shadows.
AUGUSTO ROA BASTOS, *I the Supreme.*
DANIËL ROBBERECHTS, *Arriving in Avignon.*
JEAN ROLIN, *The Explosion of the*
    Radiator Hose.
OLIVIER ROLIN, *Hotel Crystal.*
ALIX CLEO ROUBAUD, *Alix's Journal.*
JACQUES ROUBAUD, *The Form of a*
    City Changes Faster, Alas, Than
    the Human Heart.
  The Great Fire of London.
  Hortense in Exile.
  Hortense Is Abducted.
  The Loop.
  Mathematics:
  The Plurality of Worlds of Lewis.

SELECTED DALKEY ARCHIVE TITLES